Federal Bureau of I
FOIA Docume

Unidentified Flying Objects

Federal Bureau of Investigation| FOIA Documents —

Unidentified Flying Objects

United States Federal Bureau of Investigation

SECTION 1

FEDERAL BUREAU OF INVESTIGATION
U.S. DEPARTMENT OF JUSTICE
COMMUNICATIONS SECTION

AUG 11 1947

TELETYPE

FBI PORTLAND   8-11-47   1-17 PM PST   KAM

DIRECTOR   U R G E N T
    FLYING DISCS. SECURITY MATTER DASH X. ONE
____ FORMER NAVY PILOT AND PRESENTLY ____
MYRTLE CREEK, ____ OREGON, REPORTS SEEING A
MYSTERIOUS OBJECT ON TWO OCCASIONS THE
EVENING OF AUGUST SIXTH WHILE FLYING AT ABOUT
FIVE THOUSAND FEET ABOVE MYRTLE CREEK.
HATFIELD TO BE INTERVIEWED.

BOBBITT

END
5-18 PM OK FBI WASH DC GAR

Stamped:
RECORDED & INDEXED
30 OCT 1947
EX-60

STANDARD FORM NO. 64
Office Memorandum · UNITED STATES GOVERNMENT

TO: DIRECTOR, FBI   DATE: August 12, 1947

FROM :   SAC, MILWAUKEE

SUBJECT: FLYING DISCS
              SABOTAGE

Reference is made to Bureau Bulletin No. 42, Series 1947, dated July 30, 1947, Section (B), which advises that all reports concerning flying discs should be investigated by field offices.

Prior to the receipt of these instructions, two instances were called to the attention of this office concerning flying discs. One report was received July 7, 1947, the details of which are set forth in Milwaukee letter to the Bureau dated July 8, 1947, entitled, "Flying Discs or Saucers, Miscellaneous, Telephone Call from Mr. Fletcher at the Bureau at 8:30 a.m., 7-7-47." No investigation was conducted concerning this report.

The second report was received by this office at 1:20 p.m. July 11, 1947, from _____ who is in charge of the Civil Air Patrol of Wisconsin, an auxiliary of the Army Air Forces. On that occasion _____ calling from Black River Falls, Wisconsin, telephonically advised this office that an object in the shape of a disc, nineteen inches in diameter had been found July 10, 1947, by one _____ city electrician on the Jackson County fairgrounds, near Black River Falls, Wisconsin, about 3:30 p.m. The disc might be made of a substance such as cardboard covered by a silver airplane dope material. The contraption has a small wooden tail like a rudder in the back and inside of the disc is what appears to be an RCA photo-electric cell or tube. Also inside the disc is a little electric motor with a shaft running to the center of the disc. At one end of the shaft is a very small propeller. In _____ opinion that contraption might possibly have been made by some juvenile. _____ stated that he desired to return the contraption to Milwaukee and eventually turn it over to the Army Air Forces, but that the finder, _____ apparently wanted to get some publicity on his find and wanted it returned to him.

6

This information was telephonically called to the attention of Assistant Director D. M. LADD of the Bureau on July 11, 1947.

Subsequently, SAC H. K. JOHNSON telephoned Colonel ____ in charge of Counter Intelligence, Fifth Army, Chicago AC of S G-2 Headquarters Fifth Army, East Hyde Park Avenue, Chicago, Illinois, who stated he would contact ____ of Black River Falls, Wisconsin.

No further investigation was conducted in this matter.

The above constitutes the only two instances in which this office was contacted concerning flying discs. Unless contrary instructions are received from the Bureau, this office does not contemplate taking any further action in connection with the above two cases, but will fully investigate all future reports concerning flying discs.

JGF/ddc

98-0

Stamped:
COPIES DESTROYED
270 NOV 18 1964

August 5, 1947

_____
_____

Omaha, Nebraska

Dear _____

I wish to acknowledge receipt of your letter postmarked July 10, 1947, together with its enclosure.

Inasmuch as the information which you furnished is of interest to the War Department I have taken the liberty of furnishing it to that agency for their consideration.

Sincerely yours,
John Edgar Hoover
Director

WVC:mjp:rb
62-83894

Stamped:
RECORDED & INDEXED
EX-8

8

STANDARD FORM NO. 64
Office Memorandum
UNITED STATES GOVERNMENT

TO: D. M. Ladd   DATE: August 1, 1947

FROM: J. P. Coyno

SUBJECT: MRS. _____
                INFORMANT

There is attached hereto a letter received from the captioned individual postmarked July 12, 1947, concerning "flying saucers."

There is also attached a letter of acknowledgement to _____ _____ together with a letter to the War Department for approval.

It is recommended that the letter to the War Department be forwarded to the Liaison Section for transmittal to that agency.

Attachments
WVC:mjp

Handwritten:
handled separately
Stamped:
RECORDED & INDEXED

DECODED COPY

WASH FROM SFRAN   S2 8-9-47   2-50 PM   KC

DIRECTOR FBI AND SACS, SEATTLE AND PORTLAND
URGENT

FLYING DISKS, SECURITY MATTER-X. LT. COL. ____
OF G2, SAN FRANCISCO, ADVISED TODAY HE HAS NO
FURTHER INFORMATION AND THAT OUR SEATTLE
OFFICE IS IN POSSESSION OF ALL INFORMATION
KNOWN BY HIM AND IS HANDLING THE MATTER AT
TACOMA, WASHINGTON.
    KIMBALL

RECEIVED   8-9-47
8:15 PM EDST
SACS SEATTLE AND PORTLAND ADVISED
    If the intelligence contained in the above message is to be
disseminated outside the Bureau, it is suggested that it be suitably
paraphrased in order to protect the Bureau's coding systems.

Stamped:
G.I.R.-9
RECORDED
EX-45

STANDARD FORM NO. 64
Office Memorandum · UNITED STATES GOVERNMENT

TO: Director, FBI   DATE: August 8, 1947

FROM: SAC, Norfolk

SUBJECT   FLYING DISCS

Re Bureau Bulletin No. 42, dated July 30, 1947, Series 1947, wherein information is set forth pertaining to flying discs.

There is enclosed with this letter a newspaper clipping from the "Norfolk Ledger-Dispatch", dated July 9, 1947. The photograph appearing on this clipping is alleged to represent a flying disc which was observed by BILLY TURRENTINE, a Norfolk school boy, who was successful in photographing the object with his small camera.

BILLY was interviewed on August 8, 1947 by Special Agent (A) ____ at which time BILLY informed that the original negative was given by him to a Mr. BROWN of the Photo Craftsman Service, who in turn furnished the negative to the International News Service. BILLY advised that he has an agreement with Mr. BROWN whereby the latter will share equally in any profits derived from the use of the negative by commercial firms or newspapers. As of August 8, 1947 BILLY has not received any remuneration for the use of this negative.

He informed that he was sitting on the front porch of his apartment which is located on the third floor at 410 West 14th Street, Norfolk, Virginia, around noontime on July 8, 1947. He had read numerous newspaper articles pertaining to flying discs and decided to sit on his front porch in the hopes of seeing one and attempting to photograph it. On July 8, 1947 BILLY observed a large, black object moving rapidly through space proceeding from the southwest to a northeast direction. He said the black object was followed by two smaller objects which also proceeded in the same direction. BILLY explained that the objects were moving at a very fast speed which appeared to him to be much faster than the speed of an airplane, and further, that the objects appeared to be extremely high. He said that they were much higher than the average plane travels in the City of Norfolk and appeared to be above the clouds, and that a white mist followed each of the three objects. BILLY was unable to state what the black objects represented, but admitted that they could have been large balloons. He indicated that he has observed small, toy balloons flying through the air, but that definitely these were not the toy type balloons. He said that when he first observed the objects they were at such a great distance from him that it was not necessary that he raise his head in order to see them from his porch on the third floor of the apartment building. He immediately turned around to obtain his camera and estimated it took him approximately twenty to thirty seconds, at which time the discs were almost directly over his apartment and it was necessary that he stoop and look up almost perpendicular in order to obtain the photograph, which accounts for the porch railing being shown in the newspaper clipping. BILLY pointed out that the day on which he took the picture, the weather was hazy and somewhat cloudy and there was a slight breeze blowing from the southwest in the general direction of the northeast, which is the same direction traveled by the black image which he photographed.

Inasmuch as the Army authorities in the Tidewater Area of Virginia are cognizant of the above information, no further investigation will be conducted by this office in this matter.

Enclosure.

TJC:lab

62-182

Stamped:
RECORDED & INDEXED
COPIES DESTROYED
270 NOV 18 1964

FEDERAL BUREAU OF INVESTIGATION
U.S. DEPARTMENT OF JUSTICE
COMMUNICATIONS SECTION

AUG 4 1947

TELETYPE

WASHINGTON FROM NEWARK   8-4-47 5-36 PM EDST JFG

DIRECTOR   U R G E N T
   FLYING DISC REPORTED AT HACKENSACK, NJ
AUGUST   THREE,   NINETEEN   FORTY-SEVEN,   MISC.
INFORMATION RECEIVED THAT ____ AGE ____ ____ AGE
TWENTY, ____ HACKENSACK AND ____ ____ FT. DIX, NJ
ON LATE AFTERNOON AUGUST THIRD LAST SIGHTED
FROM GROUND OBJECT DESCRIBED AS FLYING DISC.
____ CLAIMED IT WAS TWO HUNDRED ____ YDS, IN AIR,
REVOLVING SLOWLY, MOVING RAPIDLY, AND NEITHER
A   KITE   NOR   A   BALLOON.   ____   TELEPHONED
INFORMATION TO HACKENSACK PD. INQUIRY BEING
MADE, BUREAU WILL BE KEPT ADVISED.
   MC KEE

RECORDED 62-83844-49
END ACK PLS
NK R 1

Handwritten:
Info. brought to the attention of ____ 8/6/47
Stamped:
RECORDED
EX-46

FEDERAL BUREAU OF INVESTIGATION
U.S. DEPARTMENT OF JUSTICE
COMMUNICATIONS SECTION

AUG 6 1947

TELETYPE

FBI PORTLAND   8-5-47   8-50 PM   HHS

DIRECTOR   AND   SACS   SEATTLE   AND   SAN
FRANCISCO   U R G E N T
FLYING DISCS, SM DASH X. RE TELEPHONE CALL
FROM MR. LADD, ONE PM TODAY REQUESTING
TELETYPE SUMMARY CONCERNING NEWSPAPER
REPORTS OF RECENT REPORTED FLYING DISCS IN
PORTLAND AREA AND A REPORTED CONFERENCE OF
ARMY OFFICIALS IN PORTLAND CONCERNING FLYING
DISCS.____ ____ THE OREGONIAN, ADVISED THAT A
CAPTAIN WILLIAM L. DAVIDSON AND LT. FRANK M.
BROWN OF FOURTH AAF HEADQUARTERS SAN
FRANCISCO WERE IN PORTLAND JULY TWENTY SEVEN
LAST AND INTERVIEWED ____ AN EXPERIENCED PILOT,
WHO HAD REPORTED JUNE FOURTEEN LAST SEEING A
FORMATION OF TEN FLYING DISCS OVER
BAKERSFIELD, CALIF. ACCORDING TO ____ THEY HAD
ALSO INTERVIEWED FOLLOWING FOUR EXPERIENCED
PILOTS WHO WERE AMONG FIRST WHO REPORTED
SEEING DISCS—____ TO ASCERTAIN THE PURPOSE OF
THE INTERVIEWS ____ CONTACTED MAJOR GENERAL
TWINING OF WRIGHT FIELD, OHIO BY PHONE AT
ALBUQUERQUE, NM, AND FROM HIM GAINED THE
IMPRESSION THAT THE AAF INSTITUTED THIS
INVESTIGATION TO WASH OUT THE DISC REPORTS,
SINCE THEY ARE DEFINITELY NOT OF AAF ORIGIN. ON
FRIDAY, AUGUST FIRST, THE PLANE IN WHICH AAF
INVESTIGATORS CAPTAIN DAVIDSON AND LT. BROWN
WERE RIDING, CRASHED AT KELSO, WASH. AND BOTH
WERE KILLED. THE WRECKAGE WAS SCREENED BY AAF
INTELLIGENCE FROM MCCHORD FIELD. THE TACOMA

NEWS TRIBUNE AND THROUGH THEM THE UNITED
PRESS PUT OUT A STORY THE PLANE WAS CARRYING
PARTS OF A DISC WHICH HAD STRUCK A BOAT OWNED
BY HAROLD DAHL AND FRED CRISMAN, TACOMA, WN.
_____ ADVISED THAT TODAY'S ISSUE OF THE
OREGONIAN CARRIES A UP STORY STATING THAT
DAHL DENIES SAYING THE METAL FRAGMENTS HE
FURNISHED WERE FROM A DISC, AND ANALYSIS OF
THE FRAGMENTS SHOWS THEM TO BE FROM A TACOMA
SLAG MILL. NO AAF INTELLIGENCE PERSONNEL
AVAILABLE PORTLAND. NO RECENT SUBSTANTIVE
REPORTS OF FLYING DISCS IN THE PORTLAND AREA.
SEATTLE VERIFY AT MCCHORD FIELD AND SAN
FRANCISCO VERIFY AT AAF HDQRTS. SF, SUBMITTING
TELETYPE SUMMARIES TO THE BUREAU. NO FURTHER
INVESTIGATION PORTLAND.

BOBBITT

END AND ACK
WA 0157AM OK FBI WA DW
SE
S OK FBI SE KLS
SF OK FBI SF NCW
DVIMSC

Handwritten:
b7C
8/6/47
cc Mr. Ladd.
Stamped:
67C
RECORDED & INDEXED
EX-30

Office Memorandum · UNITED STATES GOVERNMENT

TO: D. M. LADD   DATE: August 6, 1947

FROM :   ____

SUBJECT: FLYING SAUCERS

Special Agent ____ of the Liaison Section contacted Lieutenant Colonel ___, Army Air Forces Intelligence, inquiring about an article which appeared in the West Coast newspapers recently stating in substance that an airplane carrying recovered flying saucers crashed in route from Portland, Oregon, to Los Angeles, California.

____ advised ____ that the only information that has been received by Headquarters of the Army Air Forces is that a CIC Agent of the 4th Air Forces Headquarters, Hamilton Field, San Francisco, was killed in an airplane crash. The Headquarters of the Air Forces have been advised that he was on a top secret mission. ____ indicated that he was under the impression that the CIC Agent was either on route to or from an interview with ____ who is one of the individuals who first saw one of the flying saucers.

____ stated that the Air Forces have no additional information and will receive none until the report is received from the 4th Air Forces. ____ suggested that the San Francisco Field Office contact Colonel ___ Headquarters 4th Air Forces, Hamilton Field, San Francisco, who undoubtedly would be able to furnish the details regarding this matter which are at this time unknown by the Headquarters of the Air Forces. ____ pointed out to ____, however, that it was his belief that no flying saucers have been recovered but that it was merely an attempt to reinterview an individual who previously had reported seeing one of the flying saucers.

SWR:rnr

Stamped:
RECORDED
EX-25

Date: August 5, 1947

To: Director of Intelligence   CONFIDENTIAL
          War   Department   General BY SPECIAL MESSENGER
          Staff
          The Pentagon
          Washington 25, D.C.

Attn: Colonel ____

From: John Edgar Hoover
          Director, Federal Bureau of
          Investigation

Subject: ____

     There are attached hereto copies of a letter received from the
above-captioned individual concerning "flying discs."
     ____ letter has been acknowledged and he has been advised
that copies of his letter have been furnished to you for your
consideration.

Attachment
WVC:mjp:rb

───────────────

Handwritten:
declassified
2040
8/31/87
HM
Stamped:
RECORDED
COMMUNICATIONS SECTION
MAILED 10 P.M.
AUG 7 1947
FEDERAK BUREAU OF INVESTIGATION
U.S. DEPARTMENT OF JUSTICE

L-26
Invoice   of   Contents   from
FEDERAL   BUREAU   OF   INVESTIGATION
WASHINGTON, D.C.

Date   9-10-47   Case   Flying
                                   References   Saucer

Consigned to ——
               Estill,   South
               Carolina

List of Contents
Powered Soap Stone.

SPECIAL INSTRUCTION [illegible] Room, place date of shipment and registry number; Shipping Room, above date of this invoice; then return it to person whose name is checked in column at right. After this checked name has been initialled, invoice should be placed in administrative file.

Stamped:
COMMUNICATIONS SECTION
MAILED 7 P.M.
SEP 13 1947
FEDERAK BUREAU OF INVESTIGATION
U.S. DEPARTMENT OF JUSTICE
REGISTERED

FEDERAL BUREAU OF INVESTIGATION
UNITED STATES DEPARTMENT OF JUSTICE

To: COMMUNICATIONS
SECTION.

                              AUGUST 7, 1947

Transmit the following message
to:

                         SAC,
                         DETROIT   "URGENT"

    UNSUBS, ____ INFORMANTS, FLYING DISC, MISC.
REURTEL AUGUST 5 MATERIAL SHOULD NOT BE
FORWARDED TO FBI LABORATORY FOR EXAMINATION
BUT SHOULD BE TURNED OVER TO THE ARMY
AIRFORCE INTELLIGENCE.

HOOVER

RGF:mae

Stamped:
RECORDED & INDEXED
FEDERAL BUREAU OF INVESTIGATION
U.S. DEPARTMENT OF JUSTICE
COMMUNICATION SECTION AUG 7 1947
TELETYPE
COPIES DESTROYED
270 NOV 18 1964

Date: August 1, 1947

To: Director of Intelligence

          War Department General Staff

          The Pentagon
          Washington 25, D.C.

          Attention: _____

From: John Edgar Hoover,
          Director—Federal   Bureau   of
          Investigation

Subject   _____

    There are attached hereto copies of a letter received from the above-captioned individual concerning "flying saucers."
    _____ letter has been acknowledged and she has been advised that copies of her letter have been furnished to you for your consideration.
    Attachment
WVC:mjp

Handwritten:
declassified
2040
8/31/77
HM
Stamped:
RECEIVED & INDEXED

STANDARD FORM NO. 64

Office Memorandum · UNITED STATES GOVERNMENT

TO: DIRECTOR, FBI   DATE: July 22, 1947

FROM: SAC, EL PASO

SUBJECT: ____

             FLYING   OBJECTS   IN
             AIR

____ has come to the resident agency at Santa Fe, New Mexico on several occasions to report that she has received information concerning flying objects passing through the air. Some of the reports that she has received concern light objects seen at night which have allegedly been followed by explosions. She advised that one of such objects was reported by ____ ____ who works near Canjilon, New Mexico. She claims that others were seen near Park View and Tierra Amarilla, New Mexico.

____ called attention to clippings from various newspapers concerning "disc-like" objects seen in New Mexico and other parts of the country.

____ claims to be a student of radio waves and ray forms, and contends that the above mentioned objects may be missiles similar to those appearing over Sweden some time ago.

____ has discussed the above with officials of the Atomic Energy Commission, and has written the Secretary of War and other government officials concerning her theories. ____ for the A.E.C., has advised that officials at Los Alamos consider ____ ____ unreliable and possibly not well balanced mentally. She has mentioned to agents of this office that she was struck by lightning when a child.

On July 15, ____ came to the Santa Fe resident agency and advised that she had written to WALTER WINCHELL, promising him a story in connection with the "flying discs."

The foregoing information is being submitted to the Bureau, inasmuch as ____ has written to several government officials and Mr. WINCHELL.
62-0-3594c
FTM:GH

Stamped:
RECORDED & INDEXED

STANDARD FORM NO. 64
Office Memorandum · UNITED STATES GOVERNMENT

TO: D. M. LADD   DATE: 7/24/47

FROM: E. G. Fitch

SUBJECT: FLYING DISCS

Reference is made to my memorandum to you in the above captioned matter dated July 10, 1947, indicating that Brigadier General George F. Schulgen of the Army Air Corps Intelligence had requested that the Bureau cooperate with the Army Air Corps intelligence in connection with the above captioned matter. The Director noted on the referenced memorandum, "I would do it but before agreeing to it we must insist upon full access to discs recovered. For instance in the La. case the Army grabbed it and would not let us have it for cursory examination."

This is to advise that Special Agent ____ has recontacted General Schulgen and advised him in connection with the Director's notation. General Schulgen indicated to ____ that he desired to assure Mr. Hoover of complete cooperation in this matter and stated that he would issue instructions to the field directing that all cooperation be furnished to the FBI and that all discs recovered be made available for the examination by the FBI Agents. General Schulgen pointed out to ____ that he will from time to time make the results of the studies of his scientists available to the Bureau for the assistance of the FBI Field Offices. General Schulgen indicated to ____ that there has been a decrease in the reported sightings of the discs which might be because of the fact that it has lost much of its publicity value. He indicated, however, that he believed it necessary to follow this matter through to determine as near as possible if discs were in fact seen and to determine their origin.

General Schulgen inquired of ____ the method by which the Bureau would make the information obtained from the Bureau's inquiries, known to the Air Corps, in the Field as well as at the War Department level. Mr. ____ pointed out to General Schulgen that the best procedure appeared to be through the regular

23

established channels. It was pointed out to General Schulgen that the Bureau Field Offices maintain close liaison with the Intelligence Divisions of the various Armies as well as close liaison with the Intelligence Division of the War Department. General Schulgen indicated that he would be satisfied to receive information through this means.

General Schulgen indicated to _____ that he believed that there was a possibility that this entire matter might have been started by subversive individuals for the purpose of creating a mass hysteria. He suggested that the Bureau keep this in mind in any interviews conducted regarding reported sightings. General Schulgen stated to _____ that he would make available to the Bureau all information in the possession of the Air Corps regarding the sightings which were first reported so that the Bureau could conduct some investigation regarding these individuals to ascertain their motives for reporting that they had observed flying discs. When General Schulgen makes the information available regarding these individuals, it will be promptly brought to your attention.

SWR:rnr

Stamped:
Copies Destroyed
270 nov 18 1964
50 SEP 30 1947
RECORDED
EX-43

7/23/47

MEMORANDUM FOR D. M. LADD
RECOMMENDATION

There is attached a Bureau Bulletin to the Field for their assistance in handling this matter.
Attachment

July 30, 1947

———
———

Brooklyn 27, New York

Dear ____ :

I desire to acknowledge receipt of your letter dated July 14, 1947, and to express my appreciation to you for bringing this matter to my attention.

The information set forth in your letter has been carefully reviewed and is being maintained in this Bureau as a matter of record.

Sincerely yours,

John Edgar Hoover
Director

NOTE: ____ has been a previous correspondent with the Bu file ____ . No record could be located in the Crime Records Section indication that the correspondent might be a mental case.

STANDARD FORM NO. 64
Office Memorandum · UNITED STATES GOVERNMENT

TO: D. M. LADD   DATE: 7/10/47

FROM: E. G. Fitch

SUBJECT: FLYING DISKS

At request of Brigadier General George F. Schulgen, Chief of the Requirements Intelligence Branch of Army Air Corps Intelligence, Special Agent ____ discussed the above captioned matter with him on July 9, 1947. General Schulgen indicated to ____ that the Air Corps has taken the attitude that every effort must be undertaken in order to run down and ascertain whether or not the flying disks are a fact and, if so, to learn all about them. According to General Schulgen, the Air Corps Intelligence are utilizing all of their scientists in order to ascertain whether or not such a phenomenon could in fact occur. He stated that this research is being conducted with the thought that the flying objects might be a celestial phenomenon and with the view that they might be a foreign body mechanically devised and controlled.

General Schulgen also indicated to ____ that all Air Corps installations have been alerted to run out each reported sighting to obtain all possible data to assist in this research project. In passing, General Schulgen stated that an Air Corps pilot who believed that he saw one of these objects was thoroughly interrogated by General Schulgen and scientists, as well as a psychologist, and the pilot was adamant in his claim that he saw a flying disk.

General Schulgen advised ____ that the possibility exists that the first reported sightings of the so-called flying disks were fallacious and prompted by individuals seeking personal publicity, or were reported for political reasons. He stated that if this was so, subsequent sightings might be the result of a mass hysteria. He pointed out that the thought exists that the first reported sightings might have been by individuals of Communist sympathies with the view to causing hysteria and fear of a secret Russian weapon.

General Schulgen indicated to ____ that he is desirous of having all the angles covered in this matter. He stated that reports of his scientists and findings of the various Air Corps installations will be available in his office. He advised that to complete the picture he desired the assistance of the Federal Bureau of Investigation in locating and questioning the individuals who first sighted the so-called flying disks in order to ascertain whether or not they are sincere in their statements that they saw these disks, or whether their statements were prompted by personal desire for publicity or political reasons. General Schulgen assured ____ that there are no War Department or Navy Department research projects presently being conducted which could in any way be tied up with the flying disks. General Schulgen indicated to ____ that if the Bureau would cooperate with him in this matter, he would offer all the facilities of his office as to results obtained in the effort to identify and run down this matter.

____ advised General Schulgen that his request would be made known to the Bureau and an answer made available to him as soon as possible.

____ also discussed this matter with ____ of ____ ____ indicated that it was his attitude that inasmuch as it has been established that the flying disks are not the result of any Army or Navy experiments, the matter is of interest to the FBI. He stated that he was of the opinion that the Bureau, if at all possible, should accede to General Schulgen's request.

SWR:AJB

ADDENDUM

I would recommend that we advise the Army that the Bureau does not believe it should go into these investigations, it being noted that a great bulk of those alleged discs reported found have been pranks. It is not believed that the Bureau would accomplish anything by going into these investigations.
DML

―――――――――――――――

First Handwritten Note:

I think we should do this.
7-15

Second Handwritten Note:
I would do it but before agreeing to it we must insist upon full access to discs recovered. For instance in the La. case the Army grabbed it & would not let us have it for cursory examination.

H.

Stamped:
RECORDED

AUG 14 1947

TELETYPE

FBI SEATTLE   8-14-47   5-15   FB
                                                PM

DIRECTOR   ROUTINE

FLYING DISCS SIGHTED BY ____,
TACOMA.

WASHINGTON, SM X. REURTEL INSTANT DATE. PLEASE BE ADVISED THAT ____ DID NOT ADMIT TO ____ THAT HIS STORY WAS A HOAX BUT ONLY STATED THAT IF QUESTIONED BY AUTHORITIES HE WAS GOING TO SAY IT WAS A HOAX BECAUSE HE DID NOT WANT ANY FURTHER TROUBLE OVER THE MATTER. COMPLETE REPORT NOW EN ROUTE TO BUREAU AMSD, WHICH INDICATES PROBABLY ____ MADE THE ANONYMOUS PHONE CALL IN THE HOPE OF BUILDING UP THEIR STORY THROUGH PUBLICITY TO A POINT WHERE THEY COULD MAKE A PROFITABLE DEAL WITH FANTASY MAGAZINE, CHICAGO ILLINOIS. ____ WILL NOT BE REINTERVIEWED UNLESS ADVISED TO THE CONTRARY BY THE BUREAU.
   WILCOX

A AND HOLD PLS
9-16 PM OK FBI WASH DC GAR

Stamped:
18 Aug 26 1947.
RECORDED & INDEXED
G.I.R.
EX-67

(B) FLYING DISCS—The Bureau, at the request of the Army Air Forces Intelligence, has agreed to cooperate in the investigation of flying discs. The Air Forces have confidentially advised that it is possible to release three or more discs in odd numbers, attached together by a wire, from an airplane in high altitudes and that these discs would obtain tremendous speed in their descent and would descend to the earth in an arc. The Army Air Forces Intelligence has also indicated some concern that the reported sightings might have been made by subversive individuals for the purpose of creating a mass hysteria.

7-30-47
BUREAU BULLETIN No. 42
Series 1947

You should investigate each instance which is brought to your attention of a sighting of a flying disc in order to ascertain whether or not it is a bona fide sighting, an imaginary one or a prank. You should also bear in mind that individuals might report seeing flying discs for various reasons. It is conceivable that an individual might be desirous of seeking personal publicity, causing hysteria, or playing a prank.

The Bureau should be notified immediately by teletype of all reported sightings and the results of your inquiries. In instances where the report appears to have merit, the teletype should be followed by a letter to the Bureau containing in detail the results of your inquiries. The Army Air Forces have assured the Bureau complete cooperating in these matters and in any instances where they fail to make information available to you or make the recovered discs available for your examination, it should promptly be brought to the attention of the Bureau.

Any information you develop in connection with these discs should be promptly brought to the attention of the Army through your usual liaison channels.

Stamped:
RECORDED 78 AUG 4, 1947
252 AUG 18 1947

31

July 10, 1947

———
———

Darlington, South Carolina
    Dear ____
    I wish to acknowledge receipt of your Western Union
telegram dated July 6, 1947. Your interest in bringing this
information to my attention is greatly appreciated.
    Inasmuch as the contents of your telegram appear to be of
interest to the War Department only, I have taken the liberty of
turning this information over to that Department.

Sincerely yours,

John Edgar Hoover
Director

    cc—Savannah
NOTE: The telegram referred to "flying-discs."

Stamped:
COMMUNICATIONS SECTION
MAILED 2 P.M.
JUL 14 1947
FEDERAL BUREAU OF INVESTIGATION
U.S. DEPARTMENT OF JUSTICE
RECORDED & INDEXED

July 10, 1947

————
————

San Marcos, Texas

Dear ____

I wish to acknowledge receipt of your Western Union telegram dated July 7, 1947. Your interest in making this information available to me is greatly appreciated.

Inasmuch as the contents of your telegram appear to be of interest to the War Department only, I have taken the liberty of making the information furnished by you available to that Department.

Sincerely yours,

John Edgar Hoover
Director

cc—San   Antonio
NOTE: The telegram referred to "flying discs."

Stamped:
COMMUNICATIONS SECTION
MAILED 2 P.M.
JUL 14 1947
FEDERAL BUREAU OF INVESTIGATION
U.S. DEPARTMENT OF JUSTICE
RECORDED & INDEXED
EX-64

July 23, 1947

Westport, Connecticut

Dear ____

Your letter dated July 27, 1947, together with enclosures, has been received and I want to thank you for submitting the letter you mentioned to me.

Sincerely yours,

John Edgar Hoover
Director

BHI:pib

Stamped:
COMMUNICATIONS SECTION
MAILED 2 P.M.
JUL 23 1947
FEDERAL BUREAU OF INVESTIGATION
U.S. DEPARTMENT OF JUSTICE
RECORDED & INDEXED
EX-57

FEDERAL BUREAU OF INVESTIGATION
U.S. DEPARTMENT OF JUSTICE
COMMUNICATIONS SECTION

JUL 18 1947
TELETYPE

DIRECTOR
METAL FRAGMENTS OBSERVED AT WEST RINDGE, N.H., JULY SEVEN, FORTY SEVEN, SECURITY MATTER-X. ____, SECURITY OFFICER, M.I.T., CAMBRIDGE, MASS., ADVISED THAT TODAY HE WAS IN CONTACT WITH ONE ____ ____ OF WEST RINDGE, N.H., A RETIRED ____ OF THE NEW ENGLAND TEL. AND TEL. CO. ____ ADVISED THAT AT APPROXIMATELY THREE PM ON JULY SEVEN LAST SEVERAL PEOPLE SITTING ON A PORCH OBSERVED ON THE LAWN OF ____ ROUTE ____ WEST RINDGE, N.H., LITTLE CUP OF SMOKE, WHICH ON INSPECTION DISCLOSED SMALL BURNED ____ SPOTS ABOUT ONE AND ONE HALF INCHES IN DIAMETER ON THE GREEN LAWN. ALSO IN THE LONG DRY GRASS ON BOTH SIDES OF ROAD IN A CIRCLE APPROXIMATELY TWO HUNDRED FEET IN DIAMETER SEVERAL LITTLE BLAZES HAD STARTED AND THE FIRE ____ DEPT. WAS CALLED. FIRES WERE APPARENTLY CAUSED BY METALLIC FRAGMENTATION WHICH WERE TURNED OVER TO ____ OF MIT BY A ____ ____ OF THE TELEPHONE COMPANY. ____ HAS ADVISED ____ THAT THEIR GENERAL ____ APPEARANCE ARE SIMILAR TO THE LINING OF V DASH TWO BOMBS, WHICH HE HAD OBSERVED AT NEW MEXICO. ____ PROFESSOR ____ AN OUTSTANDING METALLURGIST AT MIT, STATED THAT THEY ARE POSSIBLY THE LINING FROM A JET TURBO PLANE. AT PRESENT TIME HE IS IN PROCESS OF ANALYZING TWO OF THESE PIECES. THESE SCIENTISTS IN ROUGHLY RECONSTRUCTING THE METALLIC OBJECT STATE IT WAS APPROXIMATELY FOURTEEN

35

INCHES IN DIAMETER, THREE SIXTEENTH OF AN INCH THICK, AND MACHINE TOOLED, AND SOME FRAGMENTS INDICATED THEY WERE BURNED AND ____ APPEARED TO HAVE BEEN SUBJECTED TO TERRIFIC HEAT. THESE SCIENTISTS ARE TREATING THIS MATTER AS CLASSIFIED INFORMATION. MR. ____ ____ AT WEST RINDGE, N.H. IS ALSO ENDEAVORING TO COLLECT ADDITIONAL FRAGMENTS AND HAS STATED THAT THE FIRE CHIEF AT WEST RINDGE HAS ALSO SEVERAL FRAGMENTS IN HIS POSSESSION. ____ INDICATED THAT THE ____ RESIDENCE IS SEVEN TO EIGHT HUNDRED FEET EAST OF THE RAILROAD TRACKS. ____STATED HE WILL MAKE THE RESULTS OF MIT RESEARCH AVAILABLE IF SIGNIFICANT. OPINIONS OF SCIENTISTS AS SET FORTH ABOVE SUGGEST POSSIBLE MILITARY INTEREST. MILITARY AUTHORITIES AT BOSTON HAVE NOT BEEN NOTIFIED.

SOUCY

HOLD

STANDARD FORM NO. 64

Office Memorandum · UNITED STATES GOVERNMENT

TO: DIRECTOR, FBI   DATE: July 18,
                                    1947

FROM: SAC, NEW HAVEN

SUBJECT: "FLYING SAUCERS"
            EDWIN M. BAILEY, JR.
            STAMFORD,
            CONNECTICUT,
            INFORMANT
            ATOMIC ENERGY ACT

For the information of the Bureau this is to advise that on July 7, 1947, ____ Stamford, Connecticut, appeared at the Stamford Resident Agent's office and furnished the following information:—

____ prefaced his remarks by stating that he is a scientist by occupation and is currently employed at the American Cyanamid Research Laboratories on West Main Street in Stamford, Connecticut, in the Physics Division. ____ further indicated that during the war he was employed at MIT, Cambridge, Massachusetts, in the Radiation Laboratory which Laboratory is connected with the Manhattan Project. ____ advised that he is thirty years of age and is a graduate of the University of Arizona.

____ stated that the topic of "flying saucers" had caused considerable comment and concern to the present day scientists and indicated that he himself had a personal theory concerning the "flying saucers". Prior to advancing his own theory, ____ remarked that immediately after the conclusion of World War II, a friend of his, ____ allegedly observed the "flying saucers" from an observatory in Milan and Bologna, Italy. He stated that apparently at that time the "flying saucers" had caused a little comment in Italy but that after some little publicity they immediately died out as public interest. ____ stated that it is quite possible that actually the "flying saucers" could be radio controlled germ bombs or atom bombs which are circling the orbit of the earth and which could be controlled by radio and directed to land on any designated target at the specific desire of the agency or country operating the bombs. He stated that one of the items of interest which he personally has observed is the fact that the saucers have been observed in Mexico City, New Orleans, Philadelphia, New York, Boston, Halifax, Newfoundland, Paris, Milan, Bologna and Yugoslavia as well as Albania. By placing a string around the globe of the earth it would be noticed that all of the above-mentioned cities form a direct orbit or circle around the earth and would be more or less in line of any path in which the saucers could be circling.

_____ further stated that he had recently talked with _____ _____, one of the owners of _____ in Glenbrook, Connecticut, and had been informed by _____ that his company is making a large powerful telescope to be used in searching the stratosphere for atom bombs.

FXM/clb 117-0

_____

Stamped:
RECORDED & INDEXED
EX-36
G.I.R.-6
COPIES DESTROYED
270 NOV 18 1964

STANDARD FORM NO. 64
Office Memorandum · UNITED STATES GOVERNMENT

TO   : Director, FBI   DATE: July 3, 1947

FROM   : SAC, Butte

SUBJECT : FLYING DISCS

Mr. ____ of the Idaho Daily Statesman, Boise, Idaho, telephonically contacted the Butte Office and asked if the FBI was checking on the flying discs reported to have been seen by many citizens. He advised that so many had reported having seen them that it undoubtedly was not a figment of the imagination. He said that these discs had been seen on July 1, 1947, in the vicinity of Trail Creek near Sun Valley, Idaho, by reputable citizens.

The writer informed ____ that this office was not making an investigation and inquired as to whether he had contacted Army and Navy officials. He said that he was inquiring of these agencies.

WGB:LB
AIR MAIL

Stamped:
RECORDED & INDEXED
EX-46

STANDARD FORM NO. 64

Office Memorandum · UNITED STATES GOVERNMENT

TO: Director, FBI   DATE: July 17, 1947

FROM: SAC, Los Angeles

SUBJECT: RECOVERY OF "FLYING DISC"

NORTH HOLLYWOOD, CALIFORNIA, JULY 9, 1947

On the evening of July 9, 1947, a report was received at the Los Angeles Office that a so-called "flying disc" had landed in the vicinity of Radford and Magnolia Streets in North Hollywood, California, the contraption being briefly described as approximately 30 inches in diameter, all metal, disc shaped, and having a radio antenna. It was reported to have burst into flames upon landing. At the time of the report the disc was being held at the Valley Fire Department in Van Nuys, California.

SA ____ went to the fire department immediately at which time it was found that a number of people had gathered including newspaper reporters and photographers who were taking pictures of the disc. Battalion Fire Chief ____ advised Agent that at approximately 10:30 P.M. an unknown woman called on the telephone and excitedly reported that the disc had dropped into her garden where it began to flame, her residence being located at 11858 Magnolia Boulevard, North Hollywood. A fire department truck was sent there and put out the flaming object with the fire hose, after which the object was taken to the fire station. SA ____ thereafter arranged to transport the disc to the office.

The device is briefly described as consisting of two convex steel discs approximately 2 feet in diameter, fused together at the outer edge and fastened together in the center by a hollow cylindrical connection. A vertical galvanized iron fin was screwed to the top of the disc, and a short length of pipe closed at one and ran from the outer circumference into the interior of the contraption. What appeared to be a radio tube was installed in the center of the top side. The contraption had a total weight of approximately 20 pounds.

At the Bureau Office a series of photographs were taken of the device from various positions, and a set of these photographs are being forwarded herewith for the Bureau's inspection and information.

The "flying disc" was thereafter turned over to Major ____ ____ A.C., G-2, Fort MacArthur, San Pedro, California, who subsequently reported that the object was definitely a hoax and under no circumstances could have flown under its own power.

Stamped:
RECORDED & INDEXED
EX-64
COPIES DESTROYED
270 NOV 18 1964

Director, FBI   July 17, 1947

Re: RECOVERY OF "FLYING DISC",

     NORTH HOLLYWOOD, CALIFORNIA,

     JULY 9. 1947

On the following day, July 10, 1947, one ____ ____ North Hollywood, reported that on this morning he was at the North Hollywood Service Station eating at which time there was considerable talk about the flying disc having been found in the vicinity. A number of what appeared to be young high school students were present and were having quite a laugh about the excitement caused by the finding of the disc. ____ stated that he received a definite impression that these young students either had themselves or knew of someone who had been working for the past two weeks making this "flying disc". ____ was unable to furnish the names of any of these young men but identified one of them who was making the statements as being employed in a Chevron Service Station at the corner of Victory Boulevard and Whitsett Street. He described the youngster as about sixteen years of age.

The above information was also furnished to the G-2 Office at San Pedro, California.

MMB:MGM
100-9099
ENC. (3)

STANDARD FORM NO. 64
Office Memorandum · UNITED STATES GOVERNMENT

TO: MR. LADD   DATE: July 10, 1947

FROM: ____

SUBJECT: FLYING SAUCERS (DISCS)
             INFORMATION
             CONCERNING

At 6.45 AM this date, SAC Hood telephonically contacted the Bureau and advised at approximately 11:30 PM, July 9, 1947, the office in Los Angeles had received information from the Resident Agent at Burbank, California, that a "flying disc" had landed in or near Burbank and had been seen to burst into flame when it landed. Further, that it had been the cause of a fire in some woods, this fire either in Burbank or possibly in the city limits of Los Angeles, which Mr. Hood could not be certain. The fire chief at Burbank had called the resident agent at Burbank and told him he would hold the disc for him.

Coincident with the information received from Burbank, the Los Angeles Office received calls from the newspapers requesting information. The newspapers stating they had called the Army Air Force Intelligence who had stated "we are not interested". According to Mr. Hood, this comment had aroused the newspapers and they stated they intended to publish this quotation and belabor same in their first issues, Mr. Hood stated that he had refrained from making any statement to the press other than to admit possession of an object and that it was being turned over to military authorities in the morning (this AM), it being Mr. Hood's opinion that he did not want any quotes in the press and certainly not one to the effect that we were not interested.

As described to him, Mr. Hood stated that the object was an aluminum disc about 2' in diameter weighing about ten pounds, painted with aluminum paint and having some sort of a radio tube in the center of the disc. This object was in possession of the resident agent at Burbank and would be turned over to military authorities (G-2) in Los Angeles this morning.

Mr. Hood's purpose in calling was to place the Bureau on notice regarding the above described object and any further information would be transmitted to the Bureau at once.

Action: None indicated.

PEW:da

Stamped:
RECORDED

July 18, 1947

———
———

Chicago, Illinois

Dear ____

I wish to acknowledge receipt of your letter postmarked July 7, 1947. The information contained therein has been carefully reviewed and is being made a matter of permanent record in the files of this Bureau. Your interest in writing as you did is indeed appreciated.

In the future should you have information which you feel might be of interest to this Bureau you might find it convenient to contact the Special Agent in Charge of our Chicago Office, which is located at 1900 Bankers' Building, Chicago 3, Illinois.

Sincerely yours,

John Edgar Hoover
Director

cc— (With incoming. There is no identifiable
Chicago information in the Bureau's files concerning the writer of this letter. Despite the fact that this letter refers to "flying discs", it is not believed that the information furnished is sufficiently important to refer to Army authorities.)

WVC:WMJ

———

Stamped:
COMMUNICATIONS SECTION
MAILED 10 P.M.
JUL 18 1947
FEDERAL BUREAU OF INVESTIGATION
U.S. DEPARTMENT OF JUSTICE

16931119R00028

Printed in Great Britain
by Amazon